Read for a Better World™

FRONT-END LOADERS
A First Look

ZELDA WAGNER

Lerner Publications ◆ Minneapolis

Educator Toolbox

Reading books is a great way for kids to express what they're interested in. Before reading this title, ask the reader these questions:

> What do you think this book is about? Look at the cover for clues.

> What do you already know about front-end loaders?

> What do you want to learn about front-end loaders?

Let's Read Together

Encourage the reader to use the pictures to understand the text.

Point out when the reader successfully sounds out a word.

Praise the reader for recognizing sight words such as *have* and *the*.

TABLE OF CONTENTS

Front-End Loaders . . . 4

You Connect! 21
STEM Snapshot 22
Photo Glossary 23
Learn More 23
Index 24

Front-End Loaders

Front-end loaders have big buckets.

Buckets pick up things.

Workers sit in the cab.

An arm moves the bucket.

The bucket has teeth. Teeth cut into the ground.

How do teeth cut into the ground?

The bucket picks up dirt.

It can also pick up rocks and sand.

Some front-end loaders move trash.

Front-end loaders can be big. Workers go up ladders to get to the cab.

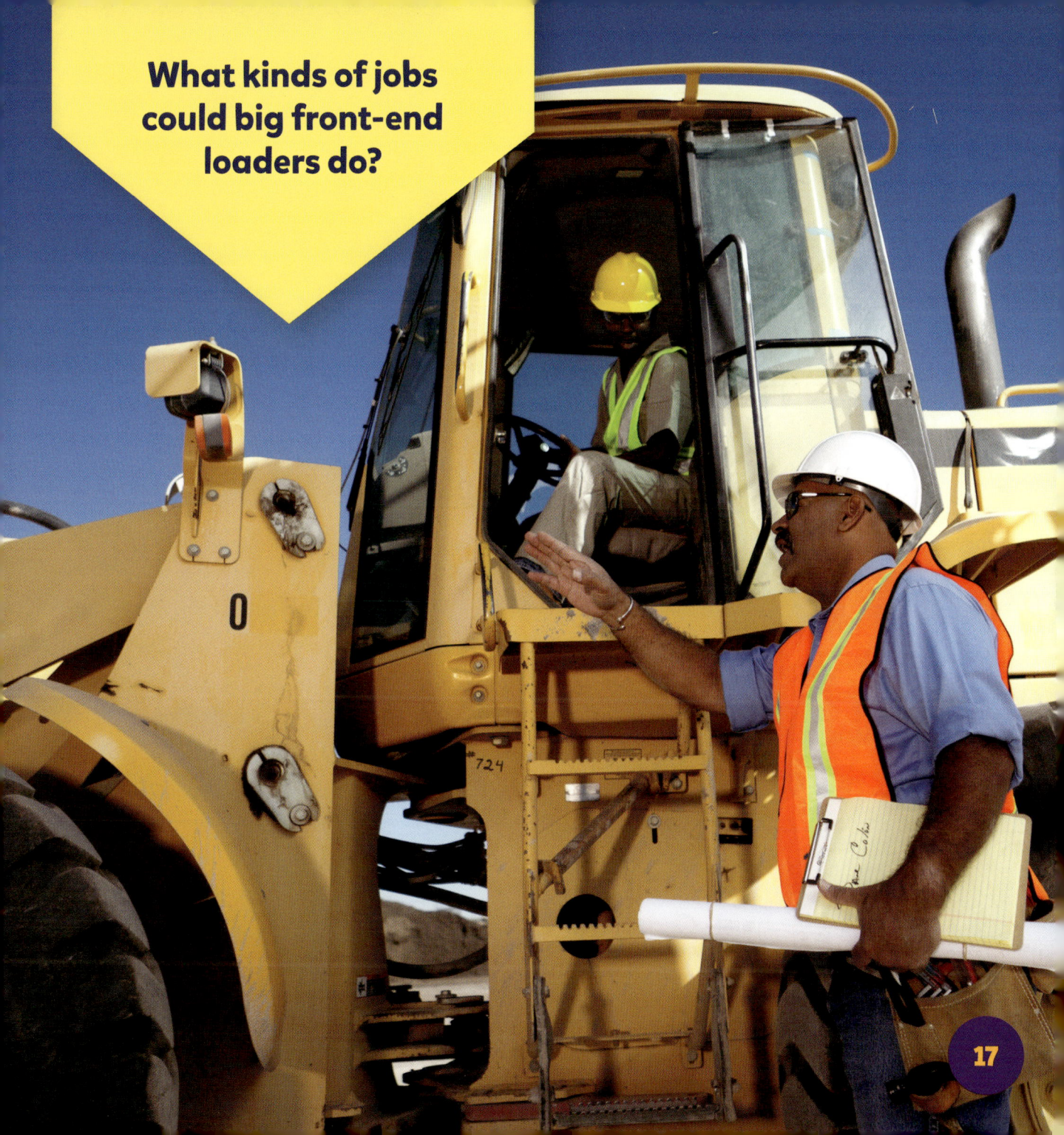

What kinds of jobs could big front-end loaders do?

Other front-end loaders are small. They work in small spaces.

What kinds of jobs could small front-end loaders do?

Front-end loaders get the job done!

You Connect!

Have you ever seen a front-end loader?

Would you want to drive a front-end loader?

How can you learn more about front-end loaders?

STEM Snapshot

Encourage students to think and ask questions like scientists. Ask the reader:

What is something you learned about front-end loaders?

What is something you noticed about front-end loader parts?

What is something you still want to learn about front-end loaders?

Photo Glossary

Learn More

Schuh, Mari. *Front Loaders*. Minneapolis: Kaleidoscope, 2022.

Wagner, Zelda. *Dump Trucks: A First Look*. Minneapolis: Lerner Publications, 2025.

Zalewski, Aubrey. *Front-end Loaders*. Minneapolis: Cody Koala, 2020.

Index

arm, 9

cab, 8, 16

ladder, 16

teeth, 10–11

workers, 8, 16

Photo Acknowledgments

Image credits: Maksim Safaniuk/Getty Images, pp. 4–5, 12; Salienko Evgenii/Shutterstock, pp. 6–7; Sorranop/Getty Images, p. 6 (bottom); Nenad Cavoski/Shutterstock, p. 8; MakaronProduktion/Getty Images, p. 9; smereka/Shutterstock, pp. 10–11; Four Oaks/Shutterstock, p. 13; 24K-Production/Getty Images, pp. 14–15; Dan Bannister/Getty Images, pp. 16–17; alacatr/Getty Images, pp. 18–19; kozmoat98/Getty Images, p. 18 (bottom); Dmitry Kalinovsky/Shutterstock, p. 20.
Cover image: guvendemir/Getty Images.

Copyright © 2025 by Lerner Publishing Group, Inc.

All rights reserved. International copyright secured. No part of this book may be reproduced, stored in a retrieval system, or transmitted in any form or by any means—electronic, mechanical, photocopying, recording, or otherwise—without the prior written permission of Lerner Publishing Group, Inc., except for the inclusion of brief quotations in an acknowledged review.

Lerner Publications Company
An imprint of Lerner Publishing Group, Inc.
241 First Avenue North
Minneapolis, MN 55401 USA

For reading levels and more information, look up this title at www.lernerbooks.com.

Main body text set in Mikado Medium.
Typeface provided by Hannes von Doehren.

Designer: Martha Kranes

Library of Congress Cataloging-in-Publication Data

Names: Wagner, Zelda, 2000- author.
Title: Front-end loaders : a first look / Zelda Wagner.
Description: Minneapolis : Lerner Publications, [2025] | Series: Read about construction vehicles | Includes bibliographical references and index. | Audience: Ages 5–8 | Audience: Grades K–1 | Summary: "Front-end loaders come in all shapes and sizes! Young readers will love learning more about parts of a front-end loader, how these construction vehicles are used, and more in this fun and informative book"– Provided by publisher.
Identifiers: LCCN 2024012745 (print) | LCCN 2024012746 (ebook) | ISBN 9798765647851 (lib. bdg.) | ISBN 9798765662236 (pbk.) | ISBN 9798765657317 (epub)
Subjects: LCSH: Loaders (Machines)—Juvenile literature.
Classification: LCC TL296.5 .W34 2025 (print) | LCC TL296.5 (ebook) | DDC 621.8/6–dc23/eng/20240402

LC record available at https://lccn.loc.gov/2024012745
LC ebook record available at https://lccn.loc.gov/2024012746

Manufactured in the United States of America
1-1010891-53346-5/30/2024